Special Days of the Year

Poppy Day

Katie Dicker

WAYLAND

First published in 2007 by Wayland
Copyright © Wayland 2007

Wayland
338 Euston Road
London NW1 3BH

Wayland Australia
Hachette Children's Books
Level 17/207 Kent Street
Sydney NSW 2000

Produced for Wayland by
White-Thomson Publishing Ltd.
210 High Street,
Lewes BN7 2NH

Editor: Katie Dicker
Designer: Clare Nicholas
Picture research: Amy Sparks
Editorial consultant: Sian Williams

Picture credits
The publishers would like to thank the following for reproducing these photographs: Abbreviations: t-top, b-bottom.
Front cover main, 13, 19, 23 – © SHOUT/Alamy. Front cover inset, 21b – www.istockphoto.com/Carsten Madsen. 3, 8, 15, 16, 27 – The Royal British Legion. 6 – www.istockphoto.com/Sandra O'Claire. 7 – © mediacolor's/Alamy. 9, 12, 17, 21t – Copyright © popperfoto.com. 10 – Photo Courtesy of U.S. Army/Spc. Harold Fields. 11 – www.istockphoto.com/Darrell Young. 14 – www.istockphoto.com/Martin Bowker. 18 – © Bettmann/CORBIS. 20 – Getty Images/Win McNamee. 22t – © Tim Graham/Corbis. 22b – www.istockphoto.com/Lance Bellers. 24 – UK Ministry of Defence/Crown Copyright/Cpl Paul Saxby. 25 – Paul Kane/Getty Images News. 26 – UK Ministry of Defence/Crown Copyright.

Every attempt has been made to clear copyright. Should there be any inadvertent omission please apply to the publisher for rectification.

British Library Cataloguing in Publication Data
Dicker, Katie
Poppy Day. - (Special Days of the Year)
    1. Remembrance Sunday - Juvenile literature 2. Armistice
    Day - Juvenile literature
    I. Title
    394.2'64

ISBN 978 0 7502 5235 5

Printed in China

Wayland is a division of Hachette Children's Books, an Hachette Livre UK company.

Note: The website addresses (URLs) included in this book were valid at the time of going to press. However, because of the nature of the Internet, it is possible that some addresses may have changed, or sites may have changd or closed down since publication. While the authors and publishers regret any inconvenience this may cause the readers, no responsibility for any such changes can be accepted by either the authors or the publisher.

Contents

What are special days? 6–7

What is Poppy Day? 8–9

Why do we have Poppy Day? 10–11

When is Poppy Day? 12–13

Why poppies? 14–15

What happens on Poppy Day? 16–17

The two-minute silence 18–19

Special music 20–21

Poppy Day in Britain 22–23

Poppy Day around the world 24–25

Why is it important to remember? 26–27

Glossary and activities 28–29

Index 30

What are special days?

We use special days to celebrate or remember an important time each year. Special days can be important to a person, a family, a town or even a country.

Every year, we celebrate the day we were born with family and friends.

People visit the graves of someone they loved.

Many families have a special day to remember someone they loved who has died. They use this day to think about all the happy times they had together.

On Poppy Day, we also remember people who have died. This event is important to many people around the world.

7

What is Poppy Day?

Poppy Day is a special day in November. It is also called 'Remembrance Day'. We use Poppy Day to remember people who have died in wars.

These people are at a special Poppy Day ceremony in London. Thousands of poppy petals fall from the ceiling at the end of the ceremony.

These British soldiers are carrying a wounded man through the mud to safety during the First World War.

Poppy Day started nearly 100 years ago. The first Poppy Day was in 1919. This was the year after the end of a terrible war, called the First World War. This war lasted for four years and over 900,000 British soldiers died.

Why do we have Poppy Day?

There have been a number of wars during the past 100 years. We now use Poppy Day to remember all of these wars.

These American soldiers are going by helicopter to fight in Afghanistan. They risk losing their lives.

We use Poppy Day to think about the millions of soldiers, sailors and airmen who have died. We also remember the families who have lost people they loved. Poppy Day is a time for families to come together to share their sadness.

These two girls are visiting the grave of their great-grandfather who died in the Second World War.

'Our great-grandfather was killed in the Second World War. We never knew him, but we know it made our family very sad.'

Jessica and Chloe

 # When is Poppy Day?

Poppy Day is on 11 November. This is the day that the First World War ended. At one time, Poppy Day was called '**Armistice** Day'. Armistice means 'ceasefire' which is what happens when people stop fighting.

These women are celebrating the end of the First World War on 11 November 1918. They worked for the British Royal Air Force.

Armistice Day was renamed Remembrance Day after the Second World War. Some remembrance **services** are held on the nearest Sunday to 11 November. We call this day 'Remembrance Sunday'.

These men fought in the Second World War. They are going to a church service to remember those who died.

# Why poppies?

Poppies grew in the battlefields after the First World War. Poppies are very beautiful flowers. Poppies are now used as a reminder of the soldiers who died.

Poppies have bright red petals, rather like the blood of wounded soldiers.

In Britain, paper poppies are sold by a charity called The Royal British Legion. This group raises money for soldiers, sailors, airmen and their families.

This woman is selling paper poppies. The money is used to help people who have suffered because of a war.

'The Royal British Legion helped to find a care home for my grandfather. He has been disabled since fighting in the Second World War and needs special care.'

Anna

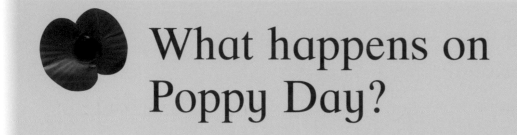

What happens on Poppy Day?

On Poppy Day, people gather together as a sign of respect for the people who have died in wars. Special services are held at **war memorials** and churches in Britain and in other parts of the world.

These soldiers are at a Poppy Day ceremony in London. Poppy petals are falling from the ceiling as a reminder of the soldiers who died.

UNITED · WE · CONQUER

IN MEMORY OF
THE OFFICERS AND
MEN OF
THE COMMANDOS
WHO DIED IN THE
SECOND WORLD WAR
1939-1945
THIS COUNTRY WAS
THEIR TRAINING
GROUND

Many people wear paper poppies to show that they remember the dead. Some people put wreaths of poppies on war memorials. A wreath is a special decoration made from a circle of flowers.

Wreaths of poppies are put on this war memorial to give thanks to the people who fought for their country.

The two-minute silence

The First World War ended at 11 am on 11 November 1918. One year later, the British King, George V, asked people to keep silent for two minutes. This was to remember the **anniversary** of the end of the First World War.

A two-minute silence has been held at Remembrance Day services at the Cenotaph (a war memorial in London) since 1919.

'Two minutes feels like a long time when no one is talking. The world seems to stand still for a moment.'

Andrew

A two-minute silence is now held at 11 am on Poppy Day every year. It is a way for people to stop what they are doing and to think about those who have died in wars.

The two-minute silence is also held at church services on Remembrance Sunday.

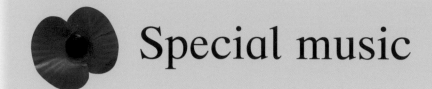

Special music

Special music is played at Poppy Day services. A piece of music called 'The Last Post' is often played before the two-minute silence.

'The Last Post' is often played on a brass instrument.

'The Last Post' has been used by the British Army for many years. The tune used to be played at the end of a soldier's working day. Now it is used to remind us of the soldiers who have died. The tune has become very famous.

These soldiers are going into battle in the First World War. Many of the soldiers died and are now buried in a war cemetery (below).

Poppy Day in Britain

In Britain, the Queen and people from the government go to a Poppy Day **ceremony** in London. This is held at a war memorial called the Cenotaph. Other important people from around the world join this ceremony.

The Queen is shown here laying a wreath at the Cenotaph war memorial in London.

In other parts of Britain, Poppy Day ceremonies take place in towns and villages. The ceremonies are held at a church or next to a local war memorial.

These children are putting wreaths on a war memorial at a Poppy Day service in their village.

'Many of the young men from our village lost their lives in the Second World War. We especially remember them and their families at this time.'

Mrs Clarke

Poppy day around the world

In the First and Second World Wars, the soldiers, sailors and airmen fighting for Britain came from many different countries. These countries also hold Poppy Day services for the people who lost their lives.

British and French soldiers are remembering those who died in the Second World War at this remembrance ceremony in Bayeux, France.

In some parts of Canada,
11 November is a public holiday.
Other countries choose a different
day to remember those who died.
In Australia and New Zealand,
for example, soldiers are remembered
on ANZAC Day on 25 April.

In 2005, these Australian and New Zealand soldiers remembered the 90th anniversary of ANZAC Day when their countries started fighting in the First World War.

Why is it important to remember?

It is easy to forget things that happened long ago. Poppy Day helps us to remember the people who have died in both old and new wars.

Today, soldiers are fighting in new wars. They will always remember the people who died trying to help their country.

On Poppy Day, we say thank you to the people who fought to protect our country. Poppy Day is a way to show that we are grateful. Remembering Poppy Day every year means that this sign of respect will continue in the future.

Older people can tell us about what it was like to live during a war.

Glossary and activities

Glossary

Anniversary – The day each year that we remember a special occasion.

ANZAC – The 'Australian and New Zealand Army Corps'.

Armistice – When people decide to stop fighting.

Ceremony – When people gather to remember or to celebrate an event.

Service – A type of ceremony.

War memorial – A statue or plaque used to remember people who have died in wars.

Books to read

• *Remembrance Day* (Start-Up History) by Jane Bingham and Ruth Nason (Evans Brothers 2005)

• *Remembrance Day* (Beginning History) by Liz Gogerly (Hodder Wayland 2003)

• *Remembrance Day* (Don't Forget) by Monica Hughes (Heinemann Library 2003)

Activities

1. Talk to an elderly relative about what they (or their parents) remember about the Second World War.

2. Visit a local war memorial. When was the memorial built? Why is there a list of names? Why was it built?

3. Choose a name from a local war memorial. Draw a picture of what you think the soldier might have looked like. Pretend to be the soldier and write a letter to your family telling them what it is like to fight in a war.

4. Look at old photographs showing soldiers from the First World War. How old do you think they are? Do you know anyone who is this age?

5. Make your own paper poppy.

6. Try to keep silent for two minutes. Use this time to think about people who have died in wars.

Useful websites

www.britishlegion.org.uk
www.poppy.org.uk
www.bbc.co.uk/religion/remembrance

Useful address

The Royal British Legion
48 Pall Mall
London SW1Y 5JY

Index

airmen 11, 15, 24
anniversary 18, 28
ANZAC Day 25, 28
Armistice 12, 28
Armistice Day (see
   Poppy Day)
Australia 25

Britain 8, 9, 12, 15, 16,
   18, 21, 22, 23, 24

celebration 6, 12
Cenotaph 18, 22
ceremony 8, 16, 22,
   23, 28
church 13, 16, 19, 23
country 6, 17, 24, 25,
   26, 27

death 7, 10, 11, 13, 14,
   16, 17, 21, 23, 24, 26

family 6, 7, 11
First World War 9,
   11, 12, 14, 18, 21,
   24, 25

music 20, 21
   'The Last Post' 20, 21

New Zealand 25

poppies 8, 14, 15, 17
Poppy Day 8, 9, 10, 11,
   12, 13, 18, 19, 20, 22,
   23, 24, 26, 27

remembrance 6, 7, 8, 10,
   14, 17, 19, 25, 26
Remembrance Day (see
   Poppy Day)
Remembrance Sunday
   13, 19

respect 16, 27

sailors 11, 15, 24
Second World War 11,
   13, 15, 24
services 13, 16, 20, 23,
   24, 28
soldiers 9, 10, 11, 14, 15,
   16, 21, 24, 26

The Royal British Legion
   15
two-minute silence 18,
   19, 20

war 8, 9, 10, 11, 12, 13,
   14, 15, 16, 17, 19, 21,
   24, 25, 26, 27
war memorial 16, 17, 18,
   22, 23, 28
wreath 17, 22, 23